PIANO · VOCAL · GUITAR

JOSH TURNER
LONG BLACK TRAIN

ISBN 0-634-08202-7

HAL•LEONARD® CORPORATION

7777 W. BLUEMOUND RD. P.O. BOX 13819 MILWAUKEE, WI 53213

Visit Hal Leonard Online at
www.halleonard.com

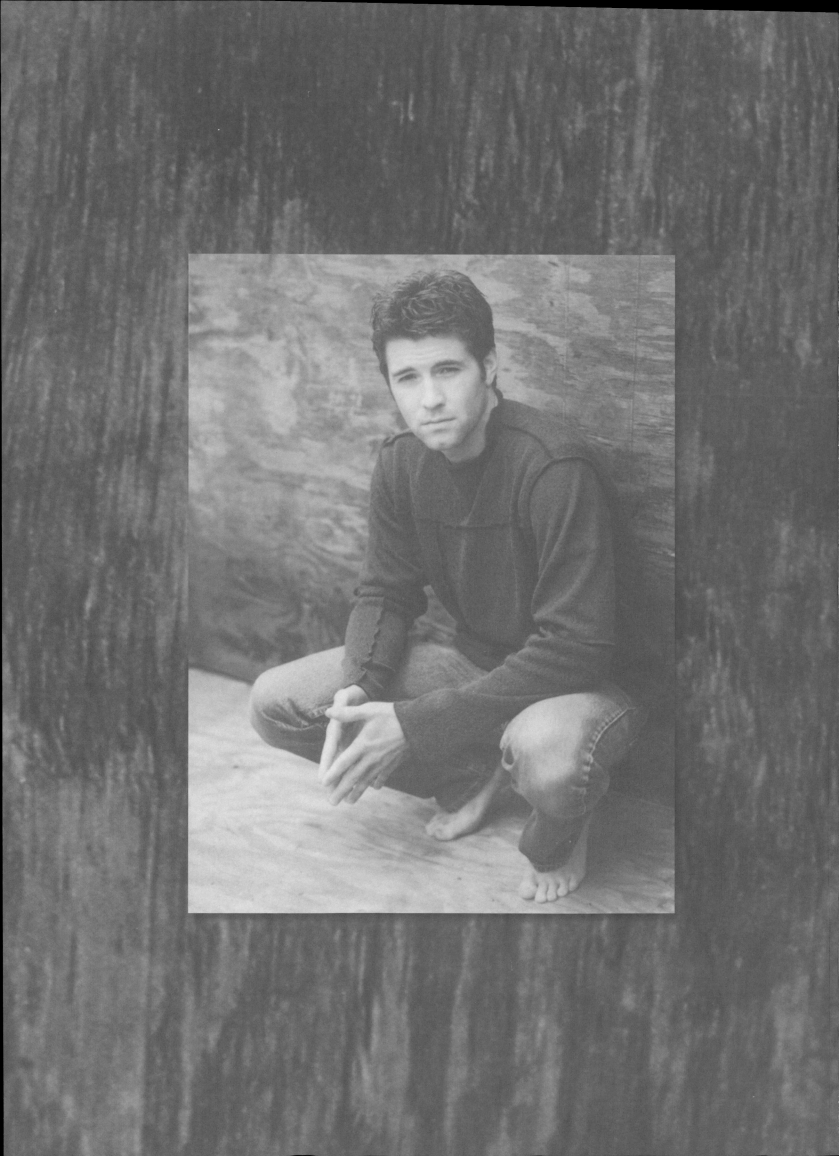

CONTENTS

LONG BLACK TRAIN

Words and Music by
JOSH TURNER

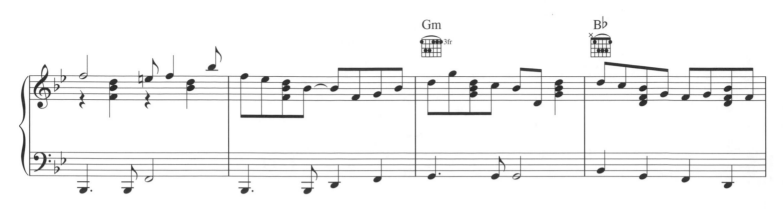

D.S. al Coda

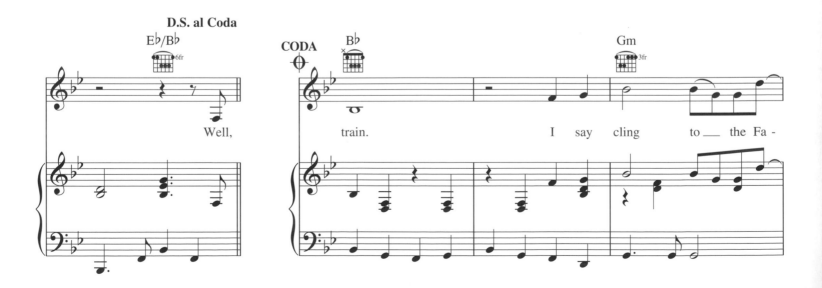

Well,   train.   I   say   cling   to ___ the Fa -

IN MY DREAMS

Words and Music by TONY MARTIN
and CASEY BEATHARD

mon - ey and __ a name. __

watch what love __ can grow. __

But in my dreams, __

Yeah, in

__ I see __ a lit - tle sky - blue house __

__ be - side __ a small __ stream, a front porch, __

__ a screen door, __ the sound of bare __ feet

WHAT IT AIN'T

Words and Music by TIM MENSY
and MONTY CRISWELL

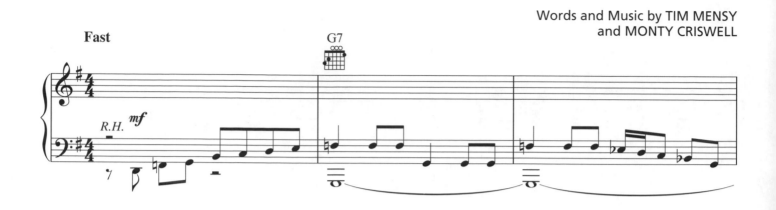

I have been a - round this ol' block be - fore.
You have say you could show me how to love.

23

I HAD ONE ONE TIME

Words and Music by DON SAMPSON
and HARLEY ALLEN

Original key: B major. This edition has been transposed up one half-step to be more playable.

JACKSONVILLE

Words and Music by JOSH TURNER
and PAT McLAUGHLIN

BACKWOODS BOY

Words and Music by
JOSH TURNER

UNBURN ALL OUR BRIDGES

Words and Music by
JAMIE O'HARA

YOU DON'T MESS AROUND WITH JIM

Words and Music by
JIM CROCE

SHE'LL GO ON YOU

Words and Music by
MARK NARMORE

59

GOOD WOMAN BAD

Words and Music by ROGER YOUNGER
and PAT McLAUGHLIN

Quickly

She was out last night ___ till way past ten, ___

Fiddle solo

same thing all ___ o - ver a - gain, ___ but with my best friend. ___

Why'd ___ she wan - na make me so ___

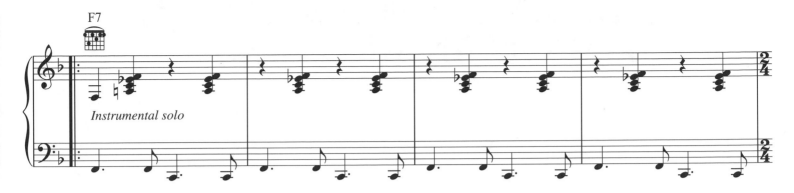

THE DIFFERENCE BETWEEN A WOMAN AND A MAN

Words and Music by
BOBBY BRADDOCK

Original key: B major. This song has been transposed up one half-step to be more playable.

But that does - n't mean ____ you're fool - ish, and you ____ know ____ I don't ____ want an - y - bod - y else. ____

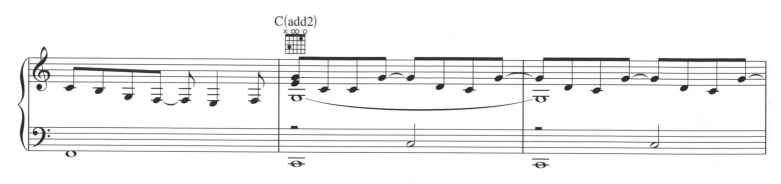

(Wom - an and _ a man.) _____

(Wom - an and _ a man.) _

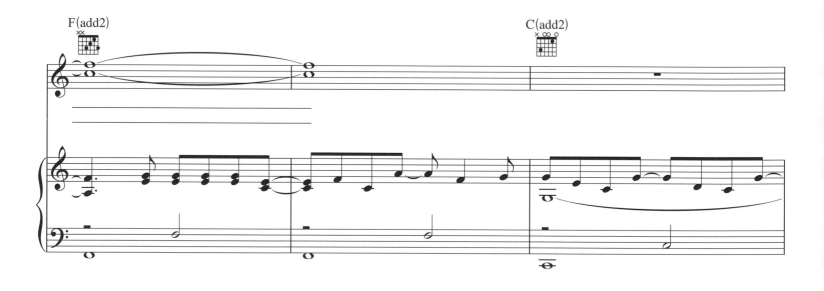

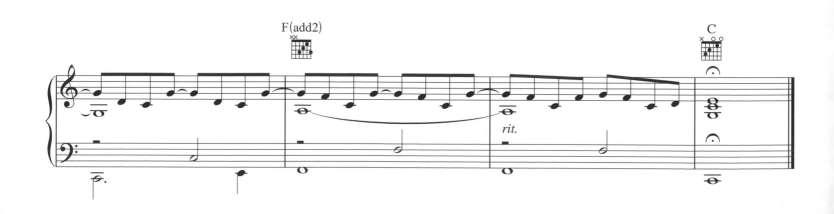

rit.